Michael Rosen

DON'T

Put Mustard in the Custard

pictures by

Quentin Blake

ANDRE DEUTSCH

For Eddie, Joe, Susanna,
Brian, Harold and
remembering Connie

First Published in 1985 by
André Deutsch Limited
105 Great Russell Street, London WC1B 3LJ

Poems copyright © 1985 by Michael Rosen
Illustrations copyright © 1985 by Quentin Blake

ISBN 0 233 97784 8

Printed in Great Britain by
Scotprint Ltd, Musselburgh

STAMP STAMP STAMP

You can hide in our house
you can make a camp
you can march all round our house
stamp stamp stamp.

TRAINERS

See me in my trainers
speeding round the house
see me in my trainers
speeding down the street
see me in my trainers
speeding to the shops.

See me in my trainers
kicking a tennis ball

see me in my trainers
kicking a hard brick wall

see me in my trainers
kicking my friends leg.

See me in my trainers
there's a hole in my toe
see me in my trainers
the sole's worn through

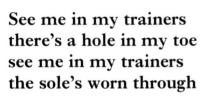

you can't see me in my trainers
they're in the dustbin.

See my trainers.

DON'T

Don't do,
Don't do,
Don't do that.
Don't pull faces,
Don't tease the cat.

Don't pick your ears,
Don't be rude at school.
Who do they think I am?

Some kind of fool?

One day
they'll say
Don't put toffee in my coffee
don't pour gravy on the baby
don't put beer in his ear
don't stick your toes up his nose.

Don't put confetti on the spaghetti
and don't squash peas on your knees.

Don't put ants in your pants
don't put mustard in the custard

don't chuck jelly at the telly

and don't throw fruit at the computer
don't throw fruit at the computer.

Don't what?
Don't throw fruit at the computer.
Don't what?
Don't throw fruit at the computer.
Who do they think I am?
Some kind of fool?

WATER

Water is what you put with
everything else
to make it not taste like water.
Sometimes you can't see it
and you have to put your hands in it
to find out if it's there.
Then people say you get soft water
and hard water.
It all feels soft to me.
Sometimes cold. Sometimes hot.

Sometimes very cold – and it goes into ice.
That's hard.
Sometimes very hot and you get steam in the bathroom.
I like it best of all
with salt
in the sea.
Though snow is good too.

DIGITAL WATCH

**Digital Fidgetal Botch
a fly got into my watch.**

**The digit digitted
the fly fidgeted.
Digital Fidgetal Botch.**

TIFFY TAFFY

**Tiffy taffy toffee
on the flee flo floor.
Tiffy taffy toffee
on the dee doe door.
Kiffy kaffy coffee
in a jig jag jug.
Kiffy kaffy coffee
in a mig mag mug.**

VIDEO

Oh video oh video
the video the diddy-o
twiddly-o the video
the video the diddle.

SOMETHING'S DRASTIC

Something's drastic
my nose is made of plastic
something's drastic
my ears are elastic
something's drastic
something's drastic.

I'M CARRYING THE BABY

Paul was three.
"Look at me," he said,
"look at me
I'm carrying the baby
look at me
look at me
I'm carrying the baby."

"Oh," said Paul,
"look at me
I've dropped the baby."

NURSERY

My mum says
once I came home from nursery
with a sulky look on my face.

"What's the matter?" she said.
I said nothing.
"What's the matter?" she said.
I said nothing.
"What's the matter?"
"I had to sit on the naughty chair."

"Why did you have to sit on the naughty chair?"
I said nothing.
"Why did you have to sit on the naughty chair?"
"Cos I was being naughty."
"Yes yes, I guessed that," she says,
"But what were you doing?"

"I was playing about at singing time,
"I wasn't singing the right things."

"What was everyone singing?"
"Baa baa black sheep."
"And what were you singing?"
I said nothing.
"What were you singing?"

"Baa-baa moo-moo."

BATHROOM FIDDLER

I'm the bathroom fiddler
the bathroom twiddler
the foodler and the doodler
the dawdler and the diddler.
I dibble and I dabble
I meddle and I muddle
when it's time for me to wash
when I know it's time for bed.

When I go up to the bathroom
to get ready for bed
I don't get washed straightaway
I fiddle and I diddle.

I pick up the toothbrush
and I bite the bristles,
I get the bristles in my teeth and I pull
I pull
I heave
I have a tug-of-war with the toothbrush
I'm winning I'm winning
yeurchk – my mouth's full of bristles.

I get the can of talcum powder
I hold it in my hand
I drop my hand down fast
and out comes a puff of powder
catch the cloud of powder
but it falls to the floor
hey, it's snowing in here.

I make mixtures in the sink
pour in the shampoo and the bubble bath
whisk it all up to make the bubbles

then I say,
"OK you Bubbles, you're finished."
At that,
I blow huge puffs of air
and the bubbles pop all over the place.

Then I stick my finger down the plughole
and scoop out the mucky stuff down there
and then I stand and dream
sucking on the sponge
and then I stand and dream
sucking on the sponge
and dream sucking on the sponge
sucking on the sponge
on the sponge
the sponge
sponge.

DON'T TELL

Christmas eve
Christmas day
don't tell mum I'm running away.

I'm afraid of Father Christmas
coming down the chimney
while I'm fast asleep
he might come and grab me.

Christmas eve
Christmas day
don't tell mum
I'm running away.

GONE

She sat in the back of the van
and we waved to her there

we ran towards her
but the van moved off

we ran faster
she reached out for us

the van moved faster
we reached for her hand

she stretched out of the back of the van
we ran, reaching

the van got away
we stopped running

we never reached her
before she was gone.

THE GREATEST

I'm the world's greatest at sport
I've won gold medals for
underwater tennis
nose throwing
elbow climbing
potato jumping
snail lifting
and computer wrestling.

I'm the world's greatest inventor
I've invented
a dog scrambler
a sock mixer
a throat cleaner
a moustache toaster
and a custard sprinkler

I'm the world's greatest.

WHO LIKES CUDDLES?

Who likes cuddles?
Me.
Who likes hugs?
Me.
Who likes squeezes?
Me.

Who likes tickles?
Me.
Who likes getting their face stroked?
Me.
Who likes being lifted up high?
Me.

Who likes sitting on laps?
Me.
Who likes being whirled round and round?
Me.

But best of all I like
getting into bed and getting blowy blowy
down my neck behind my ear.
A big warm tickly blow
lovely.

KEITH'S CUPBOARD

Have you looked in Keith's cupboard?
You ought to.
You've never seen anything like Keith's cupboard.
Let's go over to Keith's place
and look in Keith's cupboard.

So when you get to Keith's place
you say,
"Can we play with your garage?"
And he says,
"No."
So you say,
"Can we play in your tent?"
And he says,
"No."
So you say,
"Can we play with your crane?"
And he says,
"No."

So you go up to Keith's mum
and you say,
"Can we play in Keith's tent?"
And she says,
"Keith, Keith,
why don't you get the tent out?"
"OK,"
says Keith,
and he starts going over to the cupboard –
Keith's cupboard.
He opens it, and –
Phew!

You've never seen anything like
Keith's cupboard.
In it
there's trucks, and garages, and tents
and cranes and forts and bikes and puppets
and games, and models and superhero suits
and hats and
he never plays with any of it.

They keep buying him all this stuff
and he never plays with it.

Day after day after day
it all sits in Keith's cupboard.

You ought to go over his place sometime
and have a look.
Keith's cupboard.
Phew!

NIGHTMARE

I'm down
I'm underground

I'm down the Underground

Waiting

Waiting for a train

There's the platform
There's the lines
There's the tunnel
There's the lines.

I'll wait down there
Down between the lines
Waiting for the train
Down between the lines.
I'll climb down there
Down between the lines
and wait for the train
down there.

Look

Look up the tunnel look
Yes it's coming, it's coming
they say,

And it is.
And I'm between the lines.

And I can see it
See it coming
and I'm between the lines.

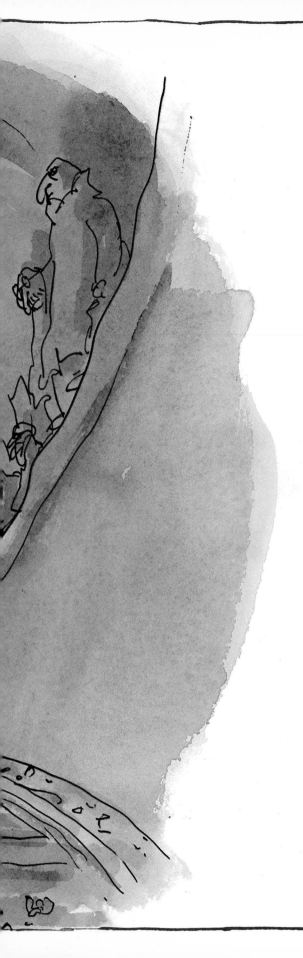

Can someone give me a
hand up?
Can't you see?

I'm between the lines
and the train's coming.
Can't you see?

I'm between the lines
and the train's coming.
Give me a hand someone
give me a hand
the train's coming
give me a hand
I can't climb up.
The train's coming
and the platform's sliding in
towards me too
with the train still coming
coming down the tunnel
the platform's sliding
sliding in towards me too.

I'm still down
Can't anyone see me
down between the lines?

Look
see
me
the train
platform
me
the train
near now
nearer now
nearer and nearer now
NOW

That's all.

BELLYACHE

I've got a belly-ache

It's right in the middle of my belly.

It's like a great big grumbling doughnut
It's like a hedgehog in there.

I've got a belly-ache
I've put a hot water bottle on it.
Didn't make it better.
I've taken really deep breaths
Didn't make it better.
I've rubbed it all over
Didn't make it better.

I want that great big grumbling doughnut to float away
I want that hedgehog to shrink.

I've got a belly-ache
and it won't go away

WHO? WHY? WHERE? WHAT?

Who invented spoons?
I don't know.
Do buffaloes eat spaghetti?
I don't know.
Why do people go to sleep?
Because – er because – er
What was the first egg in the world?
I don't know.
Where was I before I was born?
You were – er you weren't – er –
If I could turn my head round and round
    could I walk backwards looking forwards?
Could you stop asking me questions?

I'M BIG

I'm big
I'm very big
Because I'm very big
I can grab your pen
and you're scared
to try and get your pen back
because I'm big.
Very big.

But I've heard that
when people grow up
some people grow faster
than others.

This means that
when I'm grown up
you may be big
and I may be
not so big.

This is one of the things I worry about.

STUNT MAN

I say:
I'm a stuntman

I'm a stuntman
I can jump off two stairs.
He says:
Yes – jump off two stairs.
Then I jump off.
I say:
I can jump off four stairs.
He says:
Yes – jump off four stairs.
Then I jump.
I say:
I can jump off eight stairs.
He says:
Yes, jump off eight stairs.
Then I jump.
I shout:
Look at me I'm a stuntman.
He says:
Yes, you're a stuntman.

Then I say:
Now you can be a stuntman if you like
What do you want to do?
And he says:
You lie down on the floor
And I'll jump on you.

LAST WORD

Dad says:
Stop doing that:
So the boy stuck his tongue out.
Dad says:
Don't stick your tongue out at me.
So the boy says:
I'm not. I'm just licking my lips.

Later:
BANG BANG BANG BANG.
Dad says:
Stop jumping up and down up there
I can't stand the noise.
And the girl says:
I'm not jumping. I'm hopping.
Dad says:

Some people always get the last word.

SAY PLEASE

I'll have a please sandwich cheese

No I mean a knees sandwich please

Sorry I mean a fleas sandwich please

No a please sandwich please
No   No –

I'll a have a doughnut.